# GREEN THE WITCH-HAZEL WOOD

1989

# Green the Witch-Hazel Wood

POEMS BY

## Emily Hiestand

GRAYWOLF PRESS / SAINT PAUL / 1989

Publication of this volume is made possible in part by contributions of
the many corporate, foundation, and individual contributors to
Graywolf Press. Graywolf Press is a member agency of United Arts,
Saint Paul.

Library of Congress Cataloging-in-Publication Data

Hiestand, Emily, 1947-
    Green the witch hazel wood.
    (National Poetry Series)
    I. Title. II. Series.
PS3558.1345G7  1989  811'.54  88-34754
ISBN 1-55597-120-2

9  8  7  6  5  4  3  2
First printing, 1989

Published by Graywolf Press
Post Office Box 75006
Saint Paul, Minnesota 55175

ACKNOWLEDGMENTS


Warm thanks are due the Creative Writing Program of Boston University
for support and stipends that helped make this book possible.

Grateful acknowledgment is made to the following publications in which the
listed poems have appeared:


THE HUDSON REVIEW
    "This Is Something Simple," "On Nothing,"
    "Planting in Tuscaloosa."

THE ATLANTIC MONTHLY
    "Likewise," "These Are for Your Consideration"

THE NATION
    "Holly Comes From a Cold Heaven," "The Witch-Hazel Wood,"
    "Life," "Slippery Elm," "Ice Cream Music"

DISCOVERY / THE NATION
AWARD ISSUE
    "Candlepower," "Plato et Alia"

KALLIOPE JOURNAL
    "The Generous Fish," "An Old Idea," "Taking Pictures of Ducks"

PRAIRIE SCHOONER
    "Checking out the Block," "The Fence," "Route One"

SALMAGUNDI
    "Idée du Jour"

in Russian translation:
AMERICA ILLUSTRATED
    "These Are for Your Consideration"

THE NATIONAL POETRY SERIES
TENTH ANNUAL SERIES / 1989


DAVID MURA, *After We Lost Our Way*
Selected by Gerald Stern / E.P. Dutton

LEN ROBERTS, *Black Wings*
Selected by Sharon Olds / Persea Books

PAUL ZIMMER, *The Great Bird of Love*
Selected by William Stafford / University of Illinois
Press

EMILY HIESTAND, *Green the Witch-Hazel Wood*
Selected by Jorie Graham / Graywolf Press

LEE UPTON, *Constant Mercy*
Selected by James Tate / Atlantic Monthly Press


The National Poetry Series was established in 1978 to pub-
lish five collections of poetry annually through five participa-
ting publishers. The manuscripts are selected by five poets
of national reputation. Publication is funded by the
Copernicus Society of America, James A. Michener, Edward
J. Piszek, The Lannan Foundation, and the five publishers—
E.P. Dutton, Graywolf Press, Atlantic Monthly Press, Persea
Books, and the University of Illinois Press.

# Contents

"If we sell you our land, you must remember that it is sacred."
—from the letter of CHIEF SEATTLE, 1852

"What we admire in the green world is a benign selfhood.
And in one another, the ability to speak of this.
Or better, to act it out."
—*Dalhousie Farm* by WILLIAM MEREDITH

*Apple,*
*Olive,*
*Hunter*

# THESE ARE FOR YOUR CONSIDERATION

Here is the forest with very black trees
where the princess wanders with only a stone
and a silver mirror from the enchanter.

Here is a box, a gift, that rustles one night
when street lamps flicker like candles rung
around the big cement cake of our city,
the river wrapped around it, a lustrous ribbon.

Here is a mystery play with fast trains
and French doors that lead into a garden,
and locked drawers, shots and a rap at the door
and the sense that one knows and one will be

a victim, and the thin hope that someone
will untangle the riddle before the train
reaches the station where the small string-tied package
will fall into the wrong hands forever.

Here is a holy landscape, the village enclosed
by walls with helter-skelter angles so both
sides of the tiny houses and walls are visible—
a world that a god would see looking down

that day on the town—the way a god sees
both sides of all the human choices.
Here is an orange that fits in the palm of your hand
with segments like maps, and sweet, and hard.

# TAKING PICTURES OF DUCKS

It is said that when the world was young
allusions were very popular
as when Dante plucked Odysseus
from gentleman farming on Ithaka
and burned him in hell with other liars.

I need to talk to you that way
because Erasmus walks with me this winter.
He's never done that before.
We go along an icy river bank,
taking photographs of mallard ducks.

He's wearing a wonderful Dutch fur
and loves the meters on the camera.
The ducks address December en masse,
with eyes that bead from emerald heads
tight and sleek as masquerade hoods.

Wise Erasmus, tell me this:
does the window of reason shutter the world?
Once the soul was thought to be
in the pineal gland; now Shirley MacLaine
says it is spaces between everything.

That sounds like your old mystic enemy,
Luther, and the whole court of darkness.
When I get the picture from the drugstore
it is clear: ducks on a bank,
neither preening, nor hungry.

"But look," Erasmus says, a quick study,
"at the edge of your picture, a blur."

# THE GENEROUS FISH

About the sky: still blue, mysterious?
About the dead cat: was there a lap
where it was safe, and did the driver
see this tabby cat and try to swerve?
Is our cat in heaven?

Many things are known:
when to shut up, formulas for color,
that Okeephenoke means *trembling earth,*
where to find chicory weed before zealous
tractors mow down the stiff blue stands,
that poetry and science are the same,
that the miracle of fishes and loaves
is the model of perfect love.

It is not a lack of understanding—
a poise that melds from facts
so while showering or mailing a letter,
one may suddenly learn restraint.
It is not a lack of science updates,
but that every sleeping night, the world
and the fluent molecules rearrange—
a newly pleasing, newly perplexing shape.

"A different sky this morning," you say,
opening the sash. "Clouds like mackerels,
but not yesterday's mackerels." Fresh fish!
With lures we're bound for the wrinkled stream,
the plume of smoke that lifts from leafy woods
as innumerable questions blink over bowlines,
half-hitches, as in the thin pan, a sizzle—
and the generous fish shrinks to a mouthful.

# ROUTE ONE

About this time last year in March, the sky
was cold as kings; it rippled with *fiat lux*
and loomed behind trees black as blackguards.
It looked to be a philosopher's light that pried
for foothold on the cleavage face of a cliff.
Several neap tides later and having read
particle physics I know—you may already know,
but I didn't—there's no there there,
only a tendency to exist, and nature's
rock bottom fluxes to the shape of the query.

As we penetrate into the matter
she will not show basic building blocks,
only a web of relations that includes
the one who wonders in wavelike patterns.
And so to speak of particle X, gracefully
tracking across a photographic plate,
arcing cannily like frost on panes,
is at once to speak of the viewer, the one
holding the plate, the one saying pretty.

Up here in the macroscopic world,
we ride a Naples yellow van, pale as cake.
We might lob at the van some question,
but see how like a jerry-built egg it is;
the interior will be warm from sun
beading in windows with open curtains,
and what we ask is to trespass here,
on a plywood floor cushioned with our flesh,
until familiar heroes chunk the sky
and the highway darkens to huckleberry.

This is something simple—tangerine peels
shredded on the counter like rocking saucers
with butter-white insides and bits of string.
But for some peculiar reason the skins
remind me of Handel speaking of his *Messiah:*
"I did think I did see all Heaven before me."
These peels are the shavings of Heaven,
certainly not the orchard agape with music
of spherical fruits, but still, real relics,
fragrant and recently of the Garden.
I stare at them hard, up close, as though my eye
were to a keyhole. What could Handel have seen?

Perhaps what Dante saw in the blinding vision
of Paradise—light unfolding unto light—
and the one millisecond, as we might say,
of Pure Illumination. Or perhaps something
vast and geographical like the landscapes
of Frederick Church—a spectacle
of chasms and plateaus, and always a river,
a shining serpentine leading to... my God,
even the needles on the promontory pines
are absolutely realistic, with flecks
of sunset on each tip. You have to admit
there is something appealing about a gigantic vision.

But sooner or later, the visions all go
to something so brilliant it can't be described, save
as blinding light in hyperbole after hyperbole—
with cymbals, shrieks and releases of doves.
And another thing—after the levins of truth,
mystery remains, much the same as the anecdote
of the trolley and the village clock,
supposed to explain relativity, but itself
so mysterious as to require explanation.

Myself, I look at these peels and work from there.
Say these fruits and the television, the Rockies,
Hiroshima and Easter eggs and Orion,
and Peter finding arrowheads at the lake,
whooping at the luck of each sharp blue edge,
which he could hold in his hand easily
as lunch money—say all of it could be connected
by me or a greater mind—there, you'd have it!
These are pleasing skins. What nice, ruddy color.
Now they'll go in the compost, then to the garden,
and tomatoes will grow next year if the spring isn't wet.

In the mountain spurs
where grasses bulk large,
and in the deltas
where moss-like cushion plants
of the carrot family grow
near the broad bean fields,
the best known monkeys
are Red Howlers
(followed by Spiders,
Sakis, Marmosets and Nights.)
All forms are hunted.

At home in the cane
breaks is a *porco de matto,*
and a crab-eating racoon.
*Porco de mattos* invade the cities
in bands; their flesh recalls mutton.
The flesh of the sea cow
resembles roast pork.
The rattlesnake is a royal dish.
Palm beetles are relished
when fried, and scales of fish
make artificial flowers.

There are gorgeous trogons
in this home of the parakeet
and cock-of-the-rocks,
and blood-sucking vampires.
Also, there are doves
who dolorously coo
and dolphins who disport
near the rim of the basin.

Here level stretches are linked by sumptuous falls,
sufficient owing to her depths to move
colossal volumes on a steady pulse to the sea.
A typical scene: palm trees along the banks
covered with creeping parasitic plants.
Facts may help—a treacherous escapade.
This is her cycle: November to June she rises,
then falls until the end of October; at times
the river broadens—six miles, numberless canals.

One passes through a series of pongos,
shining arteries, rapids and sluggish ditches.
Imagine the widening swath of green,
columnar from mangrove thickets to snow.
Such names! Even in English, this is romance.
Say *forest, montana, prairie country, the copse.*
Aren't we away with packs and knives, quinine,
and don't we know every knot by heart.
Provisions galore—and not of the arctic persuasion,
no cheekbones bright in helmets of heavy fur.
Buckaroo, know the worst-case scenario.
The death caught here will be of fever,
vision packed close in a sweltering skull,
by degrees—filmy, spectral, turgid logic,
final slippage in the green profusion.

What gets you is the tangled jumble.
A general absence of seasonal flowering times,
a mess really, and the forest lousy with names.
Palms, acacias, laurels and tall silk cottons.
You've got your cream-nut trees, your purple hearts,
garlics of huge proportions and figs.
On the floor, swank ferns wax eloquent
and panicles of males scent the glades,

floriferous in the extreme. Plumlike blooms.
And mention should be made of the coca leaf
and leaves that kindly fan, of banana leaves
that cup the toad whose tongue is paralysis.

What is the single most important fact
near the flowering trunk of wild chocolate?
Might cocoa restore your spirit, crumbling cakes,
some morsel of convection to buttress the body
with, fleck by fleck, the sweet anchor of home.
Firm skeleton! Happy flesh that holds!

In cold logic
(true as I-beams
on a construction site
slowed by winter ice,
the building-to-be
a frame with angles
and patchy sky between
the would-be floors,
with nothing yet
in the way of water coolers
or wooly carpets cushioning,
hushing as women do, the cries,
with nothing of grained tables,
glossy as coins, cunts and leaves,
but bone solid and freezing
so a palm would stick,
with no angels nor devils
to intervene,
and in a wind that rocks
the stars in not-a-cradle,)
I try to understand logic,
just to feel that cold.

One summer, past noon, breezes shimmy
and we peer from a third-floor window.
The intersection below is a good grey nave,
calm as Newtonian space; but be alert
as though you were seeing all new,
as Balboa awakened by the Pacific.
More than one one-way sign is affixed
to the aluminum pole at a right angle.
A grey house, gabled, settles the corner
and there's greenery, including a cedar tree.
Next, a red house with a turned newel post,
white sashes, mullions, and marigolds.

Are these the right questions:
color, shape, the deployment of shadow?
Or shall we lean against these cushions, pause,
consider how to choose among the forms
of inquiry—liking intuition, liking logic.
And yet, to embrace the structural
may be to build a house of cards.
Better perhaps to persist down the block
with this one view. Later, corrections
may be made, though there is the danger
one may become wed to, say, the description
of houses and leave other approaches to wither.
The decision may be irrevocable,
made on the basis of slender evidence.
Think of Pascal and the wealth of data
pointing to some configuration of nature,
including the nature of mind, that predisposes,
so one is somehow retrieving the latent.

On faith, the next house is sparkling white
with a slate-blue roof; how like a storybook house

to have a slate-blue roof and a fence that shines
around a lot where climbing roses are climbing.
In this legacy of surveyors, plots
issue from the land like bakery numbers
to customers weighing the merits of crullers.
Now another white house, entangled with cables,
an infrastructure that lufts in swags.
And now, just roofs—red, brown, a patch of siding.
How does one return? The intersection remains:
grainy cross, a mailbox bolted to the walk.
People too who come and go.
But, lord, to get into that.

Is it a plastic brain, with pockets of air that open
and close like blue hunks of modelling clay?
When once we pulled with schooled hands,
we formed the animals, ashtrays and blobs of the '50s
that filtered through diners and sedans,
that roiled over aluminum hoods, crushing

the deco and space-age alike as the mass
seeped shapeless through vents and radio grilles.
The brain has lobes that swivel on sweet brass hinges,
kin to geodes in the vast Hall of Gems.
Thought experiments can be formed in which
pairs of electrons are sundered (one may wander

Neptune and the other fizz in a peppermint soda.)
Then the charge of particle A is changed;
then—get this—the charge of B changes too.
Simultaneously. No time for a message
to bubble over the rim of the solar system.
And so it is we know that distance is moot,

that A and B are never apart, no never.

## PLATO ET ALIA

( *for my brothers* )

Your shadow worlds and doubles
flung high as discus throwers can
are entirely beautiful to me:

the punch-out comets and stars
stuck on ceilings where heavens
skim domestically, and the schooled

models of thought like planes
my brothers glued nights at their desks,
the gooseneck lamp bent over them

all concern for their sticky fingers.
A moony lamp pooled on gliders,
fighters and on our father's shirtcards.

They used the frail woods,
balsa subject to being flattened
by wrongful, joyful leaps.

And so many are flown into walls!
Later, sturdy details are found in closets:
wings, struts, a pair of spinning wheels

and when the mind gets off its high horse
and, aching, comes to the ground—
Oh, Brother, wish I could say

female is corporeal, the firmer flesh
you desire, less given to siege.
But rather I think

one doubleness is upon
the body of women—
and a pretty one at that.

Who wouldn't choose to be
the more delicious flesh,
untroubled by hiddeness?

Our drive is from one neighborhood to another,
through suburbs where gable ends gleam,
through backsides of good towns where people
go for BP gas, where triple-deckers fly

Star Wars sheets and cotton briefs on porches,
through towns where pears and apples
and dogwoods are thickets yet unpruned,
and light crawls up each and every imploring

spindle—every limb a particular mouse grey
or dove grey and flecked with unique sap stripes.
Over a RR bridge with post-bronze-age
girders clearly demarcated in this light,

and through Scotch pines showing patches
of the brightest, coldest, bluest pond.
If ever clarity were held out to one...
this day the light divides road from roadside

and we could know the names of the builders,
how tar flows over the metal lattice, who made
the lattice and why the son of the smelter
stares at bedtime in front of a bubbling tank
as a little trunk opens and closes in the sand.

The last summer we lived in a picture book.
Our neighbor's windows glowed
and shouldered aside dark leaves
to show scenes shiny as movies.

Each window was a place
where my heart might sit on the sill
like a cat or a pie. Refrigerators
and air conditioners hummed, and if
he had been home, and if he had touched me,
I knew his hand would be warm and would bide.

Roads were built and chickens basted by day.
We paid for wars and licked commemorative stamps.
But when night wheeled on the horizon,
round and black as a massive planet,
our street was an Advent calendar with shades
opened to pieces of people who lived together:

a torso in stripes rose from a chair,
a shoulder passed plates, a head drank cola
and everyone seemed happy. Happy.
On the street, cars went gliding past,
floating jazzy wands between the elms.

Our porch overlooked the Mortali's asphalt yard,
where every night they sat in patio chairs
with their friends, lit by strings of lights,
the yellow bulbs under a blue umbrella,

the men and women fleshy and pale in flowered shirts.
Ungirdled, the moon rose over their blue umbrella.
And all through the night, the Mortali's ceramic donkey
carried geraniums toward the chain-link fence.

# VALUABLE TIMBER

The walk in the garden was meant to be a balm,
but there was a hemlock, complex with sun, three greens:
apple, olive, hunter—*none* of them true.

Stumbling on the scene, you don't invent.
Thus, as fancy turns in amusement parks
to animated figures—Goofy, Goldilocks—

at filling stations we're talking grease, just kids
plunging to our shoulder blades in ice
and groping submerged shapes in the cooler

for one skinny, starry-necked Nehi Crush.
Just so, the view from a plane is all pattern:
cloverleaf, lightbulb, lollipop drives that pop

like luck, wit or sweetness from the puzzled ground.
So it is that a valuable timber tree
bearing cones and needle leaves, sways one.

It's a beauty with shrew-brown bark like shards
over a skin that holds the cambium layer,
sapwood, and heartwood mainly for strength.

Down the nimble branches slope and splay.
Needles bristle on the stubby twigs.
The effect is that of green and curious hands

reaching almost to the ground, tempted
perennially as bees to sumptuous stamens:
touch, feel, set it down nodding, pollen-laden.

# CHEESE DOODLES

Soups secure the pantry: hearties, creams,
noodles certain as samplers stitched of X's.
All made up and got up and billowing down
down down in puckers skirting a likeness.

The nature of theatre curtains comes to me:
night lifts (this this and this happens
in a room overlooking the roof of the campanile,)
night falls. *Where were you when the world went mute?*

Remember the bit about clever brooks that sang,
foxes who spoke and trees that caught your coat,
and pointed with a knobby-knuckled twig,
though sworn to silence for the likes of you?

In the 24-hour store, generic innocence
wonders at peas frozen into blocks,
at Cheese Doodles, imagined by some soul first,
and at the children who may justly say,

"My dad invented Cheese Doodles!"
Dress for business and tell the story.
By the light of day I design with 4-color,
2 sides, on Kromekote 80-lb. paper,

with halftones, traps, no ghosting, full bleeds,
and I pray the divinities be pleased,
the way we're pleased by bougainvillaea
and finding the eye in the hard parrot puzzle.

# COSMOLOGY

It is a grand word
that seizes the welter,
molecules and doubts
the way goldfish seize
the occasion of pools—
convinced that nature
is composed, that space
is a spellbound grid of maidens,
twins, hunters and swans.

Cosmology rolls from the tongue.
It fairly bows deeply as acrobats
who grasp shaggy taut-flung ropes
cast by washerwomen, fitter for wash.
Our agile kindred can fly above
the ruffled distractions who clown below;
they can walk to the land of the Milky Way.
All the while the line is astraddle
with wooden pins, homunculus breeches
that pinch the cotton sacks and hold
the agitated and combed apparel.

Meanwhile down in the smelly arena,
a peacoat keeps you warm as toast.
Your fingers are buttered from popcorn
and all bad things stay far away
in the bleachers—rows away
from the better wooden seats.
Are the flyers not brave, and perils
subdued when they lock wrists?

Later, when the pink suits hang limp
in a wardrobe like exhausted angels
awaiting strength to go hurling
again in a mock low-lying heaven,
the spangled woman may pluck her brows,
and, save for dead give-away wrists,
seem like any woman in a slip.

Nine times out of ten
morning is metaphysical.
A pale sun rises—roll 'em—
on a multitude of cause,
auto bodies, a lot of rust,
the essential *Frank* on a wall.

Over such as these the sun
blushes again and again,
all determined glamour.
See how it rises—gently, gently,
high over the Port Authority

and over the nodding man inside,
whose copy of *Plain Truth*
slips from his grasp: splat
on the terrazzo, the slick cover
teetering away to stand alone
on the faux-marble floor.

# GOING BLIND

The trees get bare, brittle, blackgrackled,
and light just glances on the duplex walls.
Aluminum clapboards radiate a phrase:

*la forza, la forza.* A brain of twigs
complicates blue pieces of sky,
while birds, gothic, grasp the trees.

Buds easily swell to the farthest ambition.
The small sun sinks—a cold yellow bead
under loosened skeins of nimbocirrus.

This sky looms a sphinx and now it is late.
Window lamps glow in the glass;
they light wool couches, powdered cakes.

A quarter moon assumes the riddle aloft.
It is an arsenal of stars, daybreak, storms,
night.

## On Route One

It's one big mother tonight, wheeling
over the mall, over the Red Wing bar,
and the lot of twenty white trucks
parked like twenty mechanical ghosts.
Lane dividers are the brightest thing about;
a mantle of clouds shifts overhead
like someone coming to smother us with love.
The sky is the sky you know from dioramas
with wildebeests and a herd of gazelles,
with a sun about to leave us cold
in a light as far away as kings with hearts.
The trees are waving their naive arms,
hopeful as peasants in the swelling breeze.
Soon the plumbed fireplugs may start to walk.

# IN BROAD DAY

It begins with an elevator.
Some ideas of heaven
run through the city:
arches, maples dotter a wall,
a tide slaps drums,
dark comes on like flesh.
Think of Lear.
Someone—probably us—
knows to soak the swollen
feet in salts, and something
beautiful, hobbled,
is riding wild horses,
as in the peat called
the trembling earth,
leathery lids begin to gild.

What goes on here?
The situation is X,
then it fractures.
Every fact spoils some other;
soon we relent and in broad day,
near the shops and stalls,
segments cascade.
Happy ending. Happy ending.
A sour noon: shadows, sweats,
silt looped around the neck.

# IN THE CORNER

It's only the ceiling, joined to the wall.
Singular greys: polar, dove,
and from the glove-grey ceiling, a hook
swaddled in the history of paint.

Oriented by angles and shades,
the room is sealed like a shoebox.
Here we are in the corner where plenitude
grows sparse; mullions draft their shadows.

Cups and saucers drain in a rack
and blue-violet is cast to the wall.
The planes are carpenter's ideas,
the small potatoes of America

run plumb. Here it is one sags...
should this joint be wrought?
Night slums at the windows,
licking pajamas and Coldspots.

Rectangles of dark pelt the glass.
If to render truly is to become,
what thing do we do as the bowl mulls
our fruits on the laminate counter?

## THE NEWS

Cardboard boxes jumble the pantry.
There is Cream of Wheat,
and Grape Nut Flakes, and the rain
sizzles from a pleistocene sky.

There is a thud at the door;
the paper wrapped against the rain
lies layer on layer on the stoop
like milfoil, like a nest of wasps.

This is the Who What Where:
*A woman confesses to drowning*
*her daughter at the beach.*
How could she at the beach,

by the patient pearl-and-turquoise
ocean, near the tidal pools,
each one a home for hydrozoas,
winkles and sedge.

Poor drowned girl, not saved.
Why not a fisherman in a tug,
lifeguards in dayglo off duty,
coincidentally alert on the road
to the town clam joint?

## RAFT

Nowadays it is courthouses and airports
where your chart is rolled up and tied
in string, and sealed in a walnut case
with photographs and flowers.

You stand ankle-deep, beached,
by the bailiff, by the baggage,
in a swirling tide as an old geography erodes.
Even the land-locked firs fall
and lodge among pebbles and foam.

The moon illuminates a growling,
loving sea on whose surface bobs
a huckleberry raft, a sign
taut-strung between her poles.
May be a loose page from Twain.
May be a fishing boat for hire.

# REVEALING TWISTS

(bricolage from *The New York Times Book Review*)

Revealing twists, and dressed
as a meat inspector,
on the first fully modern campaign,
the issue is meat packing
and the irony of this attempt
to warm well springs of joy
with salvos at the limitations
of a world with smash hits
and endless pre-game hype.

Oh, but the beautiful savior
in gardens is plain enough;
he says: become as children again.
This tall order and the nature
of that community resemble the deeds
of a sheltered man, roughly speaking
a man greatly disappointed
and pressing the doors
of authentic faith, who may repent,
and after something of a mystery,
bolder than the last and in its sweep
laying bare self-deception
(she was almost his twin!)
would seem to be reconciled.

When one seeks to describe
what has happened, no names
are ever given, but a ceaseless
outpouring of messages, sometimes
four press conferences a day,

confusing insult with honesty
and fibbing as a mayor may fib
about cancer.
So one turns with muted voice
to largely private ends.

You learn it and you get used to it.
Still, I have hedged.
This terrible price of normality
is surely a mistake: placid surfaces,
clusters of coins, birds at the window.
Halfway across the river,
under pale skies, we nearly
come to blows about that honeyed phrase:
a new life!

# FORMIDABLE GIFT

(bricolage from *The New York Times Book Review*)

The gift is formidable, straight and elegant
in the American parlor, a momentary nostalgia
for old homes bright with disappointment,
with detailed objects and products,
with words adequate to represent the space:
deodorants, tobacco, furniture.

They had beaten drums. Now avalanches
of information set out to colonize space,
hopelessly removed from the prime-object.
They must interpret weak signals
from whatever nature throws their way
and, less than fully controlled,

a system embedded in a system,
tour the problems of the world:
the tossing of bombs, cat & mouse games,
love an event like remnant radiation.
Even more ancient are flecks of clay
in the estuaries of an evolving earth

where life as we know it today rose
to more hospitable planes,
raining down from time to time,
causing delight in our ranks.
When someone tells a story, she is fighting
for her life, and in the break and tide

of rhythm, the pulling for breath
and shrieks of words leaping to sensibility,
takes on beauty as when a colony is founded
and a portion of the virgin soil
is allotted to an auroral promise.
What harm to thrill to sudden cloudbursts,

the utmost pressure for fresh meaning?
One has smelled waxen committees,
the need for consoling fantasies,
laws against vagrancy and squatting,
what every prisoner knows
with native darkness in the public gaze.

# GIRDERS

Some of the gods we call rage
are calmed by the practices
of a democratic state.
But even this workman's
version frenzies us,
and there is yet another
and tremulous heaven,
sounding of lakes rumbling
as ice sheets nudge the shore.

I want to go there with you
as soon as possible,
but we're not going.
We're in a room
where everything
has a beautiful name.
The sky is the lead-metal
color of halls that lead
to offices and folders.
How well the girders
of this sturdy building
hold at bay a knowledge,
which we must already know
or wouldn't seek to avoid.

The problem is the dissection problem.
*Let me have at that frog.* One lays open
a tiny heart and slimy little lungs
and is sickened by bullfrogs mottled in pond water,
mating forever. Is it too much or too little love
for the world that moves one to despair
in this life about the despair of nothing after life,
which this life briefly—badly—interrupts?

It is true, nothing is unfamiliar to us,
accustomed as we are to linoleum, wool snoods,
hands in pockets feeling the working hip bone.
But nothing is not despair, nor dark, nor pain;
it is none of these, and that is the point.
So if driven by fear of nothing, despair
is a simple mistake, a bit of a joke.

And what a waste of the gaping something to think
that because it is over soon, it is a groaning
effort to haul the sun each morning, to scurry
around a pyramid of footstools, improbable beings
frantic as mimes to prop up marvels that wobble
toward drains or manholes.

And too, it's unclear that eternity
has claim to meaning, or that if we had longer—
forever say—we could do better than we do
at five in a wagon, at eighty brushing the hair
from the forehead of a new youth.
Eternity seems an unlikely place to look
for more. Those twin prongs of before and after
seem merely to hold the middle ground like skewers
on summer corn so we may bring it tidily to our lips.

In fact, we don't know that there is nothing.
All that we are and all that we aren't—it's not that.
The process of oceans grinding shells to sand
and sucking it back for bottom dwellers—it's not
even that.   Zero is our invention,
an idea for which there is no evidence.
The great metaphor of empty space is false,
full of red suns rising in every direction.
A vacuum is light. A leg severed is memory.
A child unborn is regret or relief.
An accident avoided is a picnic by the road
with Dairy Queen burgers in thin tissue wrappings
smelling of salt and blissful grease.

Except that we think of it, and on occasion,
groping for a nameless quarter, will feel the pull
of a thing beyond reckoning. But to think of it,
even to name it nameless means: *that* is not what we face.
Either our minds are famously unreliable
and we should get on with folding napkins and sheets
steaming from the iron, or our thoughts
are not aliens, rather emitted from nature like shad roe,
oxides, uranium and burls. If so, these
conceptual visions of nothing, at which we excel,
are pictures of home, to be admired more stringently.

*In*
*the*
*Field*

# MOONS IN JUNE

Cool into the window comes
the smell of cut grass and gas fumes,
old chestnuts that smack like moons-in-June.
Overhead, an arrow of light sways
small and green in a box: Go

Always everything is the same.
Honeysuckle smells like 1900.
The church spire is lit all night.
There is a street where the houses
are regular and the bushes trimmed,
the most normal street you can imagine.

People live there and you can see them
walking up the walk with a tire
or a moon-glow frisbee or
a bag of groceries—a cabbage leaf
inside flopped over a waxy carton.

At night, the air is full of rubbed wings
and chilled ice creams, the surfaces
all shown by shadows, always the same.
Windows rise on a dark bush
that throws its pointed leaves in shadow
against five and twenty clapboards.

The rubber plant has an infant leaf,
tender and mild it is. Always the same.
The only difference is sometimes you are
in love. And then you take your rosy flesh
to be the nest for some poor egg. O

the things we want to say about loving
but might just as well see: grass, flesh, air.
My own bosom rises and falls the color
of peaches—just a couple of tits heaving
in June, with crickets outside and a long arc
of a firecracker whistling in the dark.

# THE EFFECT OF LOVERS

When they kissed,
the hollows of his cheeks shone.
Sunday traffic was stacking up
at the 7-Eleven for milk.
Armando's Pizza was already
doing business,
and under the awning
a bandy-legged man
balanced on a peel of sun.

But when the grocery boy
leaned and kissed
his moon-faced girl,
against the wall
where she nested
like a ticket stub,
where light dribbled
on the parking lot
of the parish
and the funeral parlor,

I caught my breath
and so did you.
We reached into our pockets,
the deep and unlit sacks,
for whatever luck
had tossed there:
coins, a rabbit's foot,
a bullet carved to dice.
The man at the flea market
said it was carved by a soldier,
from a bullet that grazed his heart.

## April Fools

The air coaxes us as surely as the magnolias
to open in concert and melt from the mouth
of winter, salt dissolving on cheap shanks.
In common, we go soft in the head, a lapse
akin though sweet, to crimes enacted
amid the beastly desert siroccos.
Smooth as velleity giving way to motion,
when any remaining distance is too far,
the air lulls our limbs so even the butcher
calls home: *what do you say to a couple of ribs?*

# PLANTING IN TUSCALOOSA

Three women are walking in Alabama.
My mother and I help my grandmother walk
around the field where she planted and raised.
As we circle the land I think of the way
women will sometimes stroke a belly with child.
My uncle's tractor combs the deep red clay.
       Now she wears a housecoat.


Summers, I stayed with her and rode the glider
on her porch—cement painted pink.
I watched her wave a paper fan printed
with pictures of Jesus in unbelievable colors.
She waved away the sulphur smells that blew
at night from the Warrior River paper mill.
Once a man reading Sunday papers
in my bed asked me if I had page twelve;
I said I didn't have it. Then he asked
for page fifty; I said I didn't have it.
Then he asked for page seventy-three
and I said, "Go fish," and we laughed
for ten minutes and made love and laughed.
Those laughs were courtesy of my grandmother.
She played Go Fish with me for hours,
managing a dumb wedge of cards
while I was mesmerized by the distinctions
between diamonds and hearts. How
could any adult love a child enough
to play a game like Go Fish for hours?
       Now she calls us to her room.


Every summer another tree was covered
by the swarming kudzu vines that grew
taller and taller than the men with machetes.
A glass kept on her Bible magnified the word.
The women snapped beans in Sister's parlor

and watched "As The World Turns" on TV.
"Laura, was that Brian with you in church?"
Snap. Ping into the metal colanders.
I tried always to get the whole string off,
counting how many were right, two, then a goof.
How did she get the beans to snap so,
and always get the whole string off
and watch television and talk all the time.

        Now she is heaped with gladiolas.


Two women are walking in Alabama.
My mother and I walk arm and arm in her field.
The tractor harrows and dust begins to rise.
I stand ankle-deep in the field.
I am given her porcelain pitcher to keep.
Bits of clay cling to my feet.

# Making Our Garden

There are givens—pliable days
when trees and rain flow in the fields
like paint from tubes. As for us, we try too.
We built a terrace: two inches of gravel,
two inches of sand, used a leveling screed,
pavers on top in the basketweave pattern—
still, not like pictures in the Time-Life book
where edges are straight, and the gravel even.

Pictures can be so perfect.
We sawed railroad ties to the right lengths
for a bed of roses. I told him about roses:
hybrids with names, the many names of good.
You can order from a book or heft
a balled specimen from the nursery lot,
any one you want for your garden:
Alchymist, Pax, Gypsy, Joy,
Mrs. Merriweather Post, Hope.

Nothing named Doubt or Dismay or Mean
grows tinier and tinier, more and more perfect
near the center. We set out pachysandra.
It's hard to set out pachysandra.
The plant has shallow runners so you use
up too much space on the first one,
then you must twist the next one around;
by the third you're leaving root exposed
or digging up the other two.

It would have to be planned like
a Celtic knot: each runner arranged
in a geometric plot (trial and error
or use a ruler); then chalk in the plan,

revise if necessary; next dig
out the lines, some deeper than others
for overlaying; put in the plants, cover.
That's not the way we do it at all.
Yet, in time the roots entwine ingenious
under a sweet ceiling of dwarf umbrellas
about three inches off the ground.

# THE FENCE

St. Peter's rings at sunset; clouds blaze.
This could be Rome, a famous old piazza,
lights coming on in the hills.
But the children are screaming in English:
          the Celtics won!!

They kick tin and the cat named Harry;
basketballs ring on chain link
and sail over our fence into the crowd:
the May apple, the chives, uncurling and wet.

They scream, we hurl the ball back
like fans mad at the team,
throwing cups and popcorn onto the court.
The sun goes; the fervor is spent.

The children return to rooms lit by TV.
Balls roll into corners and stop.
Our affection creeps from a hedge
like the thin, quiet cat.

It is Rome. The chives live; pasta boils.
Candles and white napkins are on the table.
The E-flat Trio plays, over and over,
the part where Schubert mourns Beethoven.

Shelagh spoke of something in her kitchen
(was it war or was it Gothic art?),
lost her train, continued, circled back
until nothing of war, nothing of art remained,
only her voice, alive as she altered molecules
of beans under a ring of fluorescent light.

My friend has attracted a mate
who tells me that neural connections
in the mind are a map of consciousness.
We are carving goat cheese
from grey gauze rinds and I'm seeing
medieval cities, both sides of walled cities,
and Renaissance perspective with comely spaces.

Shelagh's mate calls her his significant other.
They smile and the haddock dances with the pot.
I worry that I am hearing voices.
I am grateful that I am hearing voices.
Maybe it is some bird in the woods.

In the morning I browse the Field Guide
of that master birder, Roger Tory Peterson.
On habitat: sea cliffs, jack pines, and scruff.
On voice: a high-pitched chorus,
*kah la a luck,* or a song that gurgles
*dear dear dear dear.*

# TALK

Bowls of blue mussels
steam on the porch,
the glisten as much as the meat
a matter of blessing.

We say grace
and then sit clumsy watching
granddaddy-long-legs stalk
the splintered rails.

We are by the patient ocean,
and a man—my husband—
talks about bait and the pitch
he is using to fix the raft,

and I see that talk itself
could ferry us away
like the smoke braiding
through the screen.

His laugh, which can pierce
my heart, avoids malice
so well I shudder.
And while we eat,

the ocean curls on the bay,
a flawless and pre-existent
beauty, like the love
each of us imagines.

April, the moon grown full.
The plot in back is full of weeds,
crusted, and crossed with sticks;
but turning the earth is a commonplace,

and often I have loved a sweating back,
the tinctures of soil down a face—
the familiar face, with his burlap sacks
of peat moss, and paper sacks of lime

and his tarragon seeds in packets, and his rue.
More than harvest, he was for the sprouts,
bent heads in rows, and for cuttings
in water glasses and slips with pallid roots.

Metaphor makes it easier to swallow.
Not everything in our garden grows;
melons sprawled in shade grow hollow.
Lank across the yard lay the hose.

But it was a real garden too,
with clematis and colonies of ants.
The earth adores her crass couplings
even beneath the trim and bourgeois hedge.

All the fancy Victorian pipes are cold.
He took the flashlight when he left,
so to read instructions on the boiler
I'll use a candle from that time we had
rosemary lamb and threw salt at the moon.
Once in our hot waving garden
a devastating blade made the air smell green.

Now—we're not talking metaphor; it is cold.
How ethereal do you want your love stories?
Maybe the angels simply need to walk.
Maybe it's need walking the face of the earth.
Our capacity for love is large; why not
love all god's children, unless the god is more

subtle, is desire in infinite schemes, appearing
to me as your eyes—deep as closets; appearing
as predilections laid down like shag carpets.
Chaucer also worried about weird angels
and quit his Knight's Tale with the Miller's,
the faint wingèd dragged bawdy to bed and made flesh

and Whirlpools, corn syrups, linoleum tiles,
as well as sedges on the winkled beach,
their languid arms angelic green on whelks.
Always the angels lay themselves down
on corrupt poor copies—trite, false, flawed—
which is to say, the world is, and full of cliché,
that under the sun everything happens again,

that oceans are blue,
that I love you.

You say to a friend, "You think you should change jobs?"
after she has said, "I think I should change jobs,"
and you mean I love you. She knows that so she says,
"Well, or else I have to talk to my boss," and you say
"You think you'll talk to your boss?" Meaning again, I love you.

I only saw the field for a minute, driving away
from his house, but all day it lies flat on my mind.
All that green. *Zzt   Zzt   Zzt   Zzt*
He has put an electric mouse device in a drawer
where I kept the whisk, spatulas, a garlic press.

He says it makes the mice so nervous they stay away.
But there is mouse evidence aplenty,
and papers, bottles—ketchup bottles, beer bottles,
ammonia bottles. "How can you live like this?"
"I miss you." "But when I was here, you weren't home."

And so on. Meaning what? I have one of his cold beers.
I don't want to add to the mess, but if I put the bottle
away will it be criticism? But if I don't maybe
he'll think I don't care so. . . maybe I should
just put the bottle in my purse. . . no, it's his bottle.

Jesus. That *Zzt   Zzt   Zzt* makes me nervous.
Where would I start to clean to get back to the wood
where I sprinkled flour and rolled out dough and cut
that magma into stars and bells? Outside it is April,
raining clean, so I leave and drive away breathing.

The field was on the side of the road, a whole wet field
of the color green shining under floodlights.
And empty. No chalk lines, base lines, 1st, 2nd and 3rd.
No pitcher's mound, no catcher's box. A pale egg-green
lime-rickey playing field that makes me thirsty.

# THE REASONABLE GIRL

There once lived a girl who was enchanted
by reason; it impressed her very much.
You often found her counting the rings of trees,
prying triangles open with X's and Y's,
watching osmosis twinkle through cells.
But when this maiden married her prince she found,
troth to tell, she loved him more than reason.

Years passed, and one day when the woman
had loved her husband through and through, he left.
He said, "Honey, you're not my type, OK?"
Something rather unusual happened then.
The mouth of a Cave came for the woman
as when a breathing quail is borne by hound

to a mistress waiting near the hunt.
Cave sang two songs—one for fruit
and one for blight—and said the woman could choose.
She thought of fruit, how she loved to take him
pears, dimpled and melting at the core,
mangoes speckled as rainbow trout...

"Choose, choose," said Cave, "choose well."
The woman who loved the man and reason chose blight.
Singing then, Cave went forth for the man
as when a hoe meets a copperhead in the field.
Now the woman's heart beats without reason,
but deep in Cave the singing never ends
and there, barehanded, she eats the rarest fruit.

# ABSENCE,

are you not the room left empty
when the wish to be saved
was deemed illusory,
and are you not the room
tended nevertheless?

Absence makes the heart grow,
makes the center a ghastly transparency
clear as our new acidic lakes
whose stoneflies and mayflies
                    disappear
whose walleyes and trout
                    disappear
whose deep channels
and shallows gain the beauty
of pools in Palm Springs.
If nature abhors a vacuum,
let her weather come.

For I have seen the world shining,
have seen her incandescent lambency flow
into the cotton fringe of thin, cheap rugs,
into the tight wound cords of telephones,
and into the epic sky. And I have seen
the corner store turn epic,
grown plump as a Russian novel,
gilt-edged and not complacent,
but finely saturated, each cornice
tracing an edge serious
as a hot-metal capital S,
the character both full and sleek.
That is, I have seen the world
coursed with love.

In the still tended rooms,
what do souls do if not long,
and what is longing if not the divine
compelling her molecular body
to tears, salt, semen, and milk.
Whatever the cause, absence, you
cause the pain of the unbeliever,
for arousal is *temenos,* and union worship.
One could shed an illusion—
though these be brilliant impersonators—
but the full-term heart
may not shake off, like some gum-ghost thought,
love that moves
as the hand moved over the water.

# MY HOUSE IN ORDER

Each thing orbits on the Formica
(itself strewn with gold like the known world)
and is the possessor of a secret.
So the proper response is astonishment
when, entering this room, you see
paper-whites blooming beside dead game,
avocados ripe on the sill with shadows.

I am familiar with these goods, the motion
of a peach to become pie, a peel
to go to leaf. Lover. Stranger.
What is rage but one more distillate
in flux, legitimate as juice and which
if fantastically bottled would also gleam.

It explodes like an old hotel... first,
rippling stone, then a long inward fall
as a structure slides from prehensile clouds.
There is a lot of twisted stuff and dust.
But afterwards, each thing is new.
Bottles are bottles—round, useful, clear.
How admirable containment is.

It allows a store of something.
Something in which to dip your fingers.
Something to smell, to break off a piece of.
To pour something splashing into a bowl.
Something to add to something.

# OLD ROSY-FINGERED DAWN

Old rosy-fingered dawn follows the storm.
Yet the leaves shudder, materialize
in blinking clusters, turned shopworn.
A novel, a romantic novel (surprise)

languishes on the standard windowsill,
a narrow slot for blockbuster pulp.
Just beyond, the weathered tin grill
prospects a pan of ashes, culpable

remains of a summer spent entertaining
the notion that marbled cuts, smoke
and lean sizzle by a painted swing
would, by fall, have cured or invoked

the true love story: satisfying plot,
the long conversation that unfolds
all summer when we're hot,
all winter when we're not.

You can't talk *Family of Man* all day.
We need a break from the sentimental
so, when five guys from Harnum Crane Co.
get the big one in gear, grey with a hook
the size of a Chevy, and all the men
for two miles come down to the shoals
to watch them block the crane footing
with 6 x 6 ties, really hauling ass
as they swing, then lower a shingled house
onto a barge headed for Rocky Neck—
the guys from the boatyard in jeans
thigh-deep in the surf to steady the barge,
a couple of summer men in khaki shorts
helping (ever notice workingmen
don't show their legs; their torsos
are pale and tender and forearms surefire
next to these scions with blond fuzz)
then yelling as if the Bruins were winning
when, after hours of maneuvers and shouts,
"whoa, hold it now, whoa, WHOA,"
the thing hanging in the balance, in thin air,
they settle the house pretty as you like
on solid flotation planks, and the painted tug
run by a fellow with muscles like melons
noses the house across the bay, where nets
of light from the constant ocean shimmer
over the shingles, and late in the day,
when they have worked the slimed pilings loose
with the crane that must go for 2K an hour,

Russ brings champagne and they slug it
around like Ripple, swigging bubbles
in the red sun, while the boatmen softly punch
the bronze men with houses and memberships
until they all stand around punching each other,

it is a good idea for a woman to say,
"Great sunset," if she is squinting into the sun,
thinking that men move a home closer
where sills may hold the usual minutiae: peaches,
safety pins, vinegars that steal the flavors
from stalks as through windows, common day lilies
shift in the glass, viscous, like syrup.

Now is the time to write the poem of your life:
a damp day that goes unspoken, a jar
of ink on a sill among slippered whelks,
the field full of bi-color corn and young corn,
and the plain brown road to the house plump
with spilt tomatoes, the red planets whirled from the cart.
A quart of peaches can fill an old compote bowl.
Little art is required. Only the bowl, a woman, the peaches.
And though in Idaho fluorescence, she will have Florentine fingers,
the long translucent tapers, and a hidden hollow palm
in which a thousand still lifes are contained.

Over centuries of Naples yellow and laborious glazes,
recall her sleeves dressed with ermine, and in the hands
of the very late Chardin, her garment grown about her arm
like a skin around a garlic.
With effort, the painter kept the molecules
of pigment distinct—this rose a woman, that tint a plant.
Yet how the dove greys of his rabbits yearn to resurrect
in the bruised-blue paper-white narcissus; how his beloved
longs to bury her flesh in the breast of a muted bird.

All this is what you must imagine.
In the room you find but the bowl, the woman, the peaches,
though in the dark bowl sleep the very rich hours,
illuminated and nicknamed time.
The name of time in truth is a multitude
that belies but a wink with a wing and a prayer
on the rosebud lips who suckle, who purse at dust and lime,
blush with grapes and, blind, attach themselves to suffer
the research of chemistry, the portions of one's age
and a wizardly, puckered withdrawal.

*She moves.*
I don't have to tell you, in a sleeveless shift.
    *She arranges her fruits.*
How like a pile of tender cannonballs, succulent warriors
turning to grass on some town green after some civil war.
    *She leaves the room.*
That is all, though she leaves like the arc of our moon,
in phases from full to new, her deckled gibbous edge
waning, confounding, clerking and blurring the line
from being to non in a motion so fine one wants a finer scope,
the pure "O" of occulus to ring her dried and radiant seas.

## MUST WE TRAIN OURSELVES
## TO BE AS DOVES

A while back I quit wearing a watch
and started keeping time differently,
like the hours that tick around a pond.
And here too, where having stood near
this credenza several thousand...

I'll say it: love is more lovely over time.
Only the moment is thought to be real,
but the here is now and then,
and see what comes into the present:
this clean bandana smells of kerosene,

of your neck and my neck, smoke,
leaves and dazzled rocks in streams.
Must we train ourselves to be as doves,
blinking pink eyes on each new moment,
astonished at the rough concrete ledge,

even at our own coo and bill.
The heart happens like a canyon, worn
breathtaking by a river at turns
a furious course, at turns a silver wander.
Now and then I roam this precinct thinking,

"Where did I stand when he brought this flowering plant?
Was I wearing a dress? Was the light orange-red
or was the shade more red-orange..."
and did I say, "How did you find the time...
how beautiful the view with crusted snow
and here, inside, these dark shining leaves."

*The
Pearly
Eye*

## A Bridge with a
## Fraternity Sign

Slanting light engineers the trellis
on which it is written: ZETA BETA
over water like Eakins on the Schuylkill,
wrinkling calm as mackerels:

silver, grey, autumnal.
Over the bridge go Skylarks and Novas;
the river wrinkles upon itself
and pylons court the water.

What looks still are stones,
iron and rivets; what looks fast
are cars, though it is all in motion
and light is in between.

The arch of the bridge
over the river that wrinkles
like mackerels—silver, grey, autumnal,
calm as Eakins on the Schuylkill—

is sought by light so the stones
are luminous, immanently so,
as jarred honey appears
to a housebound soul.

Soon the stones are dark
and the sky is red
under a pencil of spent fuel.
The Sky-Eye is about.

Later the whole of the bridge
is dark, the quarry for the keystone
moot, rivets obscured and leaves
lost from a simpler city.

On wet sidewalks at the close of fall,
leaves are flat-plastered
and full of gloss as mussel beds
that cling to rocks in summer.
These are palisade cells collapsed
from absorbing the sun,
and, looking again—
beautiful orphans undone.

Colors and shapes are telling.
This is the sweetgum leaf
of the witch-hazel wood employed
for highboys and lowboys who endured
from whaling to prohibition
and into the dens
with Fiberglas curtains that abrade.

There is comfort too;
that flat stars should quicken
the ground, like the floor
around a perfect mother's
sewing machine: each leaf
some scrap of coming to age
that settles quiet as cloth.
And the stems go in all directions;
and a rare curled blade holds water.

## SMALL SETTLINGS

A still season. The plenitude
of single cells in ponds
and marginal woods will not cease,
but on this porch all afternoon
a thin radiance courses the rail.

A motor turns. It could be
the belly of heat, so much does the air
call everything to itself.
We claim chosen wrought chairs
so there is a volume between us.
It recalls natural wonders,
two remarkable pylons.

Ice water melts. Small settlings:
how this is home and that other home
where heart-shaped leaves press the glass
is lost—not like a spoon or set of keys
that may yet dole shadows on a shelf,
or be found akimbo and placed—
oh happy day—in a safer pocket.

## THE OLD STORY

The wish that every touched thing turn gold
is chaos in morning light; logic hunkers
and plain words mean nothing over toast.
What can be recalled... straw to silk,
gilded birds, a forest with snow
and more snow falling. And morning is gone.

The youngest prince, lacking title,
forsakes the palace and soon is lost in a wood.
And the princess, who speaks to frogs,
strays from insufferable suitors, the embroidery.
Their minds are a thicketwood,
patches of light in gorgeous fretwork, given

to pity for the siblings who jostle
in coaches to their coronations, who wander
swell in lugubrious forests.
Everyone can be in the story—the elected,
the popular and well-to-do.
And it may happen in a grocery store—

every shopper with Bird's Eye peas
a princess with a pocketful of magic,
loose in a world that quavers with ash
and a grace not much involved with merit.
Soon comes an encounter with something
like death, and the character changes to stone.

But at last we hear no more of unearthly beauty;
the acrid stone assumes a mortal shape
and laundry whirls like seasons as now,
everyday, grey as bankers or blue as jazz,
we kiss our collection of toads.

## An Egg

rocks unsteadily on a surface,
causing all manner of cradles
to be ingeniously molded—
cardboard and styrofoam cartons
and porcelain cups.
Around the oval eggs in transit,
cardboard is smoothly cupped.

And still they rock to the edge
of kitchen counters
like oblivious infants.
In our world, we tell taming stories:
miraculous rescue
as when innocence is snatched
from the jaws of defeat.

This story roams the municipal halls,
the culverts and sparse unpopulated woods,
wanting passersby to play the Hero.
But in the world of a grocery egg
tumbling on a linoleum sheet,
fables improve, (e.g. turn to gold),
but do not save the egg.

And that an egg should be gold
has seemed evident good fortune.
Tell me the other story
of a simple child or fond adult
who wishes for a delicate case,
which if broken, releases
a glob of yellow, ungilded.

## BABY X

The Mother crosses
the busy street
with the Baby—
the smallest a Baby
can be out of the hospital.
Everything is dark—
the dress of the Mother,
the head of the Baby,
the hour of the Night.
And everything is pale—
the skin of the Baby,
the arms of the Mother,
the face of the Moon.

Baby X crosses
the first street of its life.
Like, it is being given
to the street.
What can Baby hear
between gas station
and sub shop?
Growls, roars, heartbeats.
Mother cuts through traffic.
She is stylish.
Baby will hear
appreciative murmurs,
honks, whistles.

This is the formation
of a new citizen.
Satellites blink
past a Marlboro sign.
Mother is skimming

the pavement in pumps.
She reaches the sidewalk
with Baby like a gumdrop.
Airbreaks squeal and truckers
slow down to see a sight
near the coffee & donut salon:
Baby is not sentimental.
This bundle is hip.

# Donna Sue Assumes Two Forms

One day Donna Sue put a luminizer in her hair, yes she did.
She got the idea from the video show, yes she did.
Donna Sue shone with the product she found on the shelf.
She made the scene all new from the lab; she pop our eye.
Nine to five doing telex, burgers, she's atrium-proof.
Everything move in her energy field and everything want to rhyme.
It's a little like a pop song, it's a little like art—
you know the next line's gonna be about the heart.
Her lover is a singer; he play electric guitar.
The man she's crazy for is what you call a rock star.
(Girls, she recommends a rock star.) He sings to her:

> Donna Sue, Donna Sue
> It's a luminized you
> Oh Donna Sue, Donna Sue
> It's a luminized you.

By the time she was thirty, Donna Sue had developed nearly
magical powers. Because news of this comes to you in a poem,
the slow deft untangling of what magical powers are in an
urban setting, which you would discover in a short story, will
be telescoped. Imagine the call to her mother Irene in a
Louisville trailer park, the visit from Michael who works
nervously at a downtown law firm, the averted scene about
overdone veal at The Pleaides, the way light, squirrels and
yellowed blinds in store windows call themselves toward her,
and be satisfied with this fact: one evening Donna Sue fed
twelve friends with a single package of Lean Cuisine. Everyone
found the food delicious, imaginative, and as they strolled
away from Donna Sue's third-floor walkup, into a mapled
night, down streets with windows like mild pumpkins, they
thought—to a person—it was some enchanted evening.

## MEMORIAL DAY,
### LEAVING FOR ROME

Come tomorrow, we'll be European
but on this last day in America,
let us marvel as smoke plumes rise
from the calm, green ponds of yards,
as once on the isle of Aiai, the Big O
saw smoke lift through the trees
near the heart of Circe's household.

Handsome maples vignette a porch:
geraniums, awnings, an outdoor carpet.
This sky smells of rain, a wind like skirts.
Gloxinia spill from their boxes
and in our new world, normally a city,
people roast corn, meat and potatoes.
They sing the spangled anthem, get blousy
on beer, and horse around the pit.

## FLORENCE

We are suffered in the garden
among orianders prickled with sun.
A restoration is underway;
the city is under a fine green net
rigged on a scaffold held with bolts of brass.
Laborers drill the stucco palaces.
Underfoot, the brown magnolia leaves,
like lizards, scramble the peastone path,
and on the surfaces of pools
revolve in a stunned flotation.

# POSTCARD

Having a wonderful time here
Sunday morning at the Reservoir,
where water awaits begonias and washing machines.

A leaf shredder has been this way.
Wish you were here—the cracks on the paths
are gilded with crinkled sumac and maple powder.

New rivulets and tributaries
leap from the blacktop layer, lurid,
like infrared pictures from space, a watershed:

we are wearing seven-league boots;
we are running in a fairy tale
on a photograph of the earth.

First a cheerful warning:
the standard gate-arms lower with bells.
Now here it comes.
One is mildly surprised by this freight
cheek-by-jowl with our houses,
as well as the hard, poor places.

This gritty train lumbers the crossing,
pulling a slow concern for the hapless.
In the open cars are gunnies of wheat
and oranges, the sacks lumpish
as "going dead." That was when,
younger, the wish for utter still pulled
on skinny limbs and one was sunk
with love and suspicion—both lodged
deep as the turtle in the slag pond,
in her vast accreting shell.
To feel the cool suck of mud
and then, at the last, to spring away...

The young can toy with going dead.
We watch carefully now, idling.
One drubs a molded wheel.
One strains to admire the train
vanishing in two-point perspective.
Was it then a brush with lassitude?
Lift up your arms, be lifted up ye arms.
Our sun-limned legs and elbows
have been run ragged, but quick hands
may ever pluck from under the wheels
even the least coin of the land,
pressed to a smoother face,
more to our liking, gently struck.

# L I F E

On a walk, a stone walk
whose visage is an aggregate
bleached in the sun,
each slab is hard and docile,
a magnanimous square
sown with mica chips
one of which could be
the final decimal point
of data in the collecting jar
of the world, the bit
that (easily as a firefly
closes its acrid wings
and holds the round
and glassy wall) causes
one to trust in solid ground.

Home from the walk,
say, "I'm home,"
and the kitchen door—
bevelled in lavender tubes
of light elicited by carpenter's
ideas of how to coax the sun—
destines you, someday,
to choose a box of fancy soaps:
three cakes like three sisters
wrapped in pleated tissue,
sealed with gold paper seals.
Each egg of lavender released
is plump and smooth in the palm,
the weight the weight of promise.

## At the Pavilion, Newport

Pavilions abound in this old whaling town.
This one inhabits an ocean park,
a little sward with a marginal wood
aflutter with Pearly Eyes,
the satyr butterfly whose wings
hold four dark purple eyes.
The columns of the pavilion are doric,
old and upright as men and women
who once braced their limbs to bear
great pallets of wheat at harvest.
There are children at play on the floor,
where the old stones must seep
a little through their cotton jeans.

Down by the limestone seawall
a statue holds a looking glass,
one fixed arm flung to the waves
where beyond the bronze man,
day sailors come about
neat and clean as napkins.
Still, we want the unreckless hero
knowing something of stars,
of hardware and conversation
to despook the night at anchor
with halyards rattling.

These columns are smooth carved,
like the boon of an apple,
like the full, clear face
we long to give the world,

and yet I am thralled
as across the surfaces, light
goes lily, dove, charcoal,
and fails to undo the dark.
Can we breathe on the earth,
heroic and mild as the weak
dancing flight of the Pearly Eye?

# WHO CALLS OUT

Who carries a brown egg in a spoon
across the clay floor in morning,
steam flowing like a comet tail.

Who cools it in clear water,
takes it in a white china bowl
to the beloved for breakfast.

Who calls out on the night
of the gibbous moon
to come to the garden and see.

Who stands in the damp matted grass
near the new planted turnips
and points to Cassiopeia.

# QUIET WOMAN

When Quiet Woman comes,
she fills my ears
with morning glories.
Morning glories
grow out my ears—
big blue trumpets
in those soft canals.

My hearing is better
than a geezer's,
but the dog howls
when the telephone rings.
I do not answer
with a flower in my ear.

I hear only wind
and the scuttle of trinkets
she tosses my way:
garters, crosses, scars,
glimmers and brass.

### 1. *At a Physics Convention*

Here the air is a soup of leptons and quarks,
the new vocabulary as yet barbaric
and trembling as plastic on conveyor belts,
unrubbed by greasy and worried thumbs.
Also there is a Table of Contents including:
Officers and Executive Committee, Directors,
Past Presidents, Committees, the Hall of Fame,
Honorary Members, an alphabetical Index
to all Members, a Calendar, a Code of Ethics,
and a Form to change old listings.
This is published as a service to Members.

### 2. *In Another Part of the City*

Intelligent beans are heaped on pale Formica;
old sixties songs like "Long Time Passing" playing
and no one here to hear, no one but bright beans
akimbo green in jackets. It sounds unlike
the radio church blaring toward Christ—
onward marching blessing—or television static.
You never heard this tune. Go catch the cactus
singing—a plant that blooms but sparsely
when arroyos are up to their earlobes in monsoon.
It's the undine, mab, nearly impossible strain,
stored in walls, thought to rise like the moon.

When slippery elms in summer leaf plunge
(as later maples draining sugar will plunge),
honest rhapsodics, into a spate of talk,
sap turns to wine, and the plein air
to a thronged cafe where everyone gestures
(except one languid Beauty.)
Sun renders each blade a raconteur,
each leaf in the tossing branches, a tongue,
a provocative one to cull replies
about the coming event of night.

Burning bushes are natural phenomena:
roses of sharon in fencerows,
fox grapes and swollen concords,
privet hedges in boxcar trim, clapboards,
bless them, horizontal if not plumb,
and man-made signs dazzled on the pavement.
One says "Let's Go Bowling!"
Let us bowl then, you and I,
by the lambent fast-food emblems.
Under the tossing alley trees,
we can cheer the moon, sliced pale.
She climbs through a joinery of limber straws.

# No More Ornate

We walk a mudflat,
and to our surprise
there are similes
stuck in the flats.
A pike has sides shiny
as a beaded purse.
The sun, setting,
cleaves a pine tree
red and black,
lurid as nightclubs.
Pin oaks rustle
like Russian sleighs,
and a calliope
of children steams
across the field.
Assimilated trinkets,
talk no more ornate
than the tails
of lyretails
and tiger barbs,
devised for heaven
knows what reason.

# HOLLY COMES FROM
## A COLD HEAVEN

Holly comes from a cold heaven
and enters our city on flatbed trucks.
Here honest artificers wait

with ribbons and cunning snowmen.
On the river that winds through town,
people skate in aching parabolas.

Handel is once again transported
and in our house we loosen exemplary
boxes of oranges riddled with cloves.

Outside the frosted windows, cans
are frozen to the streets, amute
as we are, aghast at the sun and dazzle

of fact fragmenting: high rose windows
and the Apollo Belvedere seem
mere islands of belief that drift.

By sags and rises kitchen string lifts
popcorn. Hallelujas worry the walls.
But lustre fools our language; if someone

should say, "Merry," we *are*, greenhorns
like holly, soaking up sun, shining,
prickling, according to natural law.

## LIKEWISE

The pond is like a mackerel skin tonight,
the mackerel like a beaded evening bag.
This is like that, that is like this, oh,
let's call the whole thing off and take it straight:
nothing is like anything else.
Even the parrot and the apish ape
mirror, mimic and do like—unmatched.
To begin: algae, abalone, alewife—
each the spitting image of itself.
Likewise beetles (potato, scarab and whirligig.)
Nothing even comes close to barrel cactus,
nothing is more original than a bog,
more rare than the cougar and crane—
save all the above named.

I've never seen anything like it: dust bowls,
deer, the descent of man and estuaries,
flakes of snow (no two alike), fire,
flax, gannets and gulls.
Honeybees and the Hoover Dam
are unique—there is nothing like a dam.
Ditto inbreeding, ice ages, industrialization,
Joshua trees, lagoons and the law
that to liken a lichen is tautological.
Indeed, the rule of diminishing simile holds
that all of these are idiosyncracies:
the Leakeys, legumes, maize, marsupials and moose.

Virtually nothing is extraneous here—
not orchids, ooze, pampas nor peat.
This is the world of plenitude and power—
every bit of it out of this world:

the rain and rattlers, sperm, swamps and swans.
As now we inch toward an end—vectors
and a winter that figures to be like no other,
say the selfsame earth is to your liking,
and let us continue—yeast, yuccas, zoons,
all things like, beyond compare.

# CANDLEPOWER

When a dealership opened (Grand!)
or carnival came into lots outside town
not far from the dump, we children,
thin and growing up southern godly,
were taken to the big deal by searchlight—
the lamps loose scissors large
as tools of the weird sewing sisters,
their candlepower good to forty miles
in fog from the insolvent river.

The scissors of light searched our skies,
and trees, and on the rise, the transformers
and towers that rung the Tennessee Valley.
The long beams of light flushed the faces
of newel posts in town, briefly ripe,
to the color of pumpkins.

They betrayed themselves at last
to be drawn on flatbed trucks—
kettle-drum lights bolted to a rig.
But I loved a cheap stunt
and when we rode through the night,
the lamps that called us to Chevrolets
confirmed in my ignorant heart
that somewhere Heaven was searched
by a Mother Ship
with a round and radiant technology.

# ICE CREAM MUSIC

Five o'clock of late July,
our part of the planet cools
and motors give way
to inescapable clinks
of forks on plates—
no humbler sound—
attention on a bite of beef.

Enter the ice cream truck:
still playing a music
of eucalyptus floors,
mirrors with blackamoors
melted down to silver coins,
tousled in a dazzle
along a gurgling stream,
the tune, the tune
that came around the corner,
prelude to ring games—
delicate strains.

I assume the truck et al.
because all I hear is the music,
lifting from the speakers' intentions.
Music calls for children
but my window is open,
so beribboned liquors climb
over the placid sills, climb
over the summer-cracked sills,
ardently Victorian, and babble
to me, enchanted skeptic,
that brooks are wound around
our stoops still courted by shade maples
masking the ever-ruddy sun
from runs of rocky hollows.

Lush and benign, the sound
looks for a child with sixty cents,
but it is loose as teasle and worts
caught in woolen cuffs,
the escapes to roadside scruffs—
called *escapes* by naturalists
in the vocabulary for transport.

This is a voluntary music,
old, already old-fashioned
four and thirty years ago
in nineteen fifty-four
when town bandstands
were set aside bright white
on islands of green,
and the word "bikini"
was about to be big; it comes
from a lumbering truck
through sheet-metal walls
dimpling under the weight
of a lurid selection board.
I'm not buying the confections,
but hear O! hear the tape
rolling with cargo
of cream and sugar for sale,
onto another sweet-toothed street
where little ones want a *bombe*
or a chocolate rocket.

A boy (your thin boy
all limbs and a cotton tunic
over his cage of ribs)
is silly with some joke,
twisting on the leather seat
of his papa's van.
One glimpses his life,
which is, like all lives,
lucky or unlucky,
impossible to say.
It would take as long to say
as for the boy to find
all his sandcrabs,
torture or save them,
and wear his dinner jackets
along the cold sand
and speak of saving crabs
to a date (how he took them
in the cup of his hands
and how after that
it was all videos
and with enough quarters
he would save the planet.
She laughs.)
And later for him to lie
in his room, lank,
unable to say his desires.
Elsewhere Billie Holiday
turns a noun into a verb:
*"And if I cabaret on Monday,*
*ain't nobody's business if I do."*
Going faster—the salad, thunder,

the housefly on the rim of a drink
and heels that click on the pavement
and shades that blow around light bulbs
conspire—which means
*"to breathe together."*
The legs click away to their house
where stockings are surely pulled
from pale calves,
and the boy is driven to many lessons.
But the singer spins around
and around. *Turntable.*

# H A L F  R H Y M E

Half rhyme, 1/2 scientific thought,
partial bushwack at moral tone,
50/50 rant and social observation,
semi-ecstatic nature walk,

6 of one half-hum. Not the zeal
that sunders the swollen neutron,
nor the lay that divides the lawns
and creases courtlands in the fields,

but more than half made with glue—
unguent, solvent, what have you
that acts upon the too many halves
and halves not, but renders for laughs,

for a breath, a split second or two,
the whole ball of wax, half true.

This little line got tongue-tied.
This little line is dumb.
This little line is cockeyed.
This... miracle! A blossom in the stream—
gibble gabble jaw jabber a priori *blossom*.

Weird how the word works.
BLOSSOM. Brainstem, blowsy,
two syllables, two lips oratorical.
Say Bloss some. Blah, blah, sum.
The blossom drums da Dum within the seed.

Hush, petal ear. Hear the earth's ambition
creak—orchard to orchard.
Nova, Nova. It is a blooming universe.
Here is a line that opens like a starfish,
like a starfish eating sea blossoms,
embracing the blossoms and slowly,
deliciously, building the body of the world.

## MANITOULIN ISLAND

We have come so far north,
we are in another country.
There is no language here,
so we listen to the loons,
and when we cease to say *loon,*
or *tree,* these return
as though the yank of speech
had never singled them out—
like the balding producer,
not above the seduction of power,
who points to a shapely pair of gams.

Nor are we wrong to pluck
from the salt-strewn night a *star,*
to wrap our tongues around a burning mass
so unlike earthly ceramics, unable
to mingle with the slope of a breadbox
or the cooled agate knobs in a kitchen.
The sky is a fondled, spilled necklace
unspoken; the cygnet we say, the swans,
the charioteer—and the world is restrung.

The night is full of gasses and rocks
long construed by our lips to be pilots
and faith for hopeless lovers,
to be honest minions who serve our pleasure
(with the ordinary mix of smiles and tucking-in
of blankets and plans to burn our house down),
their given names helpful as pocket knives.
How else shall we cut wedges from the cheese,
the great whey wrapped in gauze,
and who among us will say which is finer—

the uncubed wheel or the snap of the blade:
*Tree. Star. Loon. Leaf.*

If we beheld a tracery, so like a hand,
that defines the belly of a leaf
and were undrunk on the liquor of tongues,
a silence would come
silent as the bluff on Manitoulin
where we fingered the edge and, shrunken to a crouch,
received the wordless plain of pine and fir.
Pines and firs in a supple sea of needles on spars,
no telling where that forest goes, or how far.

## ON A NIGHT LIKE THIS

Prawns are heaped on the bank,
their bodies the shape of commas.
We sleep by a river that washes
the spine of our Mother.
Her sky is dark like a cellar,
her moon a scimitar,
beaten to helpless silver.
On a night like this
she stays up late,
telling the story
of when she was young,
before we were born.
She remembers
that her woods were green.
Her hair, she says, was long,
and shining—and then,
she laughs and laughs.

# A BOY AND HIS BALL

Some kid is bouncing
a big rubber ball—
sounds hollow.
What is bouncing
but letting it fall,
to gravity and all that,
knowing return for a fact.

The rubbery world
with heat-sealed lines
rebounds to his palm,
so a boy may keep his gaze
on the scruff of park,
on the chain-link
nets of the neighborhood,
or on the sky, crazed
by the arms of elms

into the skies of pictures
with river banks grazed by Guernseys
and a fishing boy whose oiled image
lifts off the old linen in hunks.
A boy bouncing a big rubber ball
may keep his gaze elsewhere.
He may do as he pleases,
assuming the ball returns.

# BIRTHDAY PARTY, AUGUST 9TH

The uninvited one lingers
after my guests have gone.
She walks with me
about the wickets in the lawn,
where wooden balls sprawl
like a model of planets—
some close by, one far away
near the pine tree.

We brush a solid lilac,
the great hearted plant breathes
on our thin cotton dresses.
On the party table, ribbons curl
around glass plates with melted lakes.
The sun explodes in the lemonade.
"So pretty, so pretty," she murmurs,

and I think she has forgotten,
and I smile at the sweet debris
on my garden table. Now she says,
"Listen—cicadas in the pine are calling,
*Nagasaki, Nagasaki, Nagasaki.*"

## An Old Idea

I too love the old idea of earth.
Mother. One outrageous tit
or more properly, miraculous bosom

suckling her raw materials, her ores,
tendons and pelts, her wiggling blue-green algae.
And how sweet, when the rococo bargains

called cities soot and weary, to recall
that we squirm from a warm female,
that when we crumble, it is She who wails

and She to whom we may return.
Yet so long as male prevails, the earth,
to endure, must change her sex

and stern gather power for the sake of power,
an earth who if He holds you close,
holds you rough to a rough face.

If ever you have seen a knuckled pine
grasp a ledge, water tumble
cold minerals in spring, steelheads

gum the edge of their galaxy for flies,
or a long scalp of bending timothy hay
take a rolling hill to be its own,

you may be prepared to say, like the whore
to Solomon, I'll give this baby away.

# IDÉE DU JOUR

*What can be done?*

One idea a day, like an apple,
or better, a stitch in time,
or time permitting, embroidery.

*Who is qualified?*

Bees of pilgrims, ladies' garment workers
in close swarms, even roustabouts
pressed into service to mend torn flaps,
a dropping hem, a heavy wool that wants
a heavy gauge—anyone with good ears
who hears whistling through tears in the cloth.

*What will they use?*

Every dimestore has palettes of spooled thread,
wound and popped into precision-dimpled cases,
before which industry may be forgiven this once
if it snaps suspenders and rocks on its heels.

*What will they sew?*

What if the world were a tent, nylon
or canvas, and every inch a voluminous idea:
the idea of hemp, of slippery elms,
the mistaken ideas of pointillists,
platonic haunches of the horse,
long-winded storms, scudding garrulous,
and the fleet wit of clouds.

# THIS IS THE WAY I DO IT

In an election year I favor this
for a summertime activity:
go stand at your own screen door
in the migrant Okie apron way
during mid-day sun or near dusk
when satellites show up in the sky.

Your eyes swim in and out of focus
so the dizzy grid interchanges with leaves,
lawns, the concrete walk, what have you.
Like a fine mesh of reason it is:
a maple is twenty grids wide, though hazy
and if you back up—maybe thirty.

Nothing surreal flies in American air.
The fringed old leaves just wave
like our idea of girls in Lotus Eater
air so sleepy all the houses are going
to sleep, like a child's book closing
fat golden pages on vanilla cupcakes.

Everyone knows staring out the porch,
when bowls of new potatoes are on the table,
is true grit, so—this is the way I do it:
"Mr. President," I say, wiping my hands
on the apron, which is yellow with flowers,
"the enemy lives here, so far as I can see."

And by this time he is looking at it too:
soft-focused and bright beyond the pine
and the yard which eventually curves
into the shape seen by the astronauts,
some of them forever changed.

# PIANO

Outside is the ocean,
and she is combing
for blind spots.
She is all a heroine
should be; she
cannot stop dreaming.
There is one
shortage after another:
groceries, water,
medicine.

Her foremothers hoped
for amicable neighbors
for greens and birds
as they pitched
their canvas tents in camps.
She cannot stop dreaming
of canvas luffing,
of the sound in the wind,
nor of the stalks
whose veins number
as the multitude
of wretched on the earth.

Combing her keys,
(she has been seated
at a piano)
      Be seated thou
she cannot stop
playing the tune
of the rag and bone woman
who tinkers with things,
her meal ticket won
in a fledgling science.

## SALT & PEPPER

On the day to clean the collection,
a giant of a woman comes
and washes the dusty folds of ducks
and magi and all things
in the collection—which is everything
you can think of in the world
made into salt and pepper shakers.
Not only is the cleaning woman
a giant, she is a witch.
All that she touches is washed lifesize.

Two whimsical girls twirl two
parasols and sit on steamer trunk.
They are going to travel!
One is blond and one is brunette.
Between them lies a well
and in the well, a tiny spoon.
The trunk is soundly made
with a fine keyhole, better made
than some monumental curios:

the White House and the U.S. Capitol—
rendered with porticos and columns
but poorly molded, wrought more
like lumps than offices of a State
that gleams on behalf of a people.
Here a woman should want
to clarify the very cast of the land,
daubing acid gently in the corners.

There is a figurine bed, a double,
with a sleeper not asleep,

her black dots of eyes surprised
or pleased. She is Salt and she lies
on her side, the sheet on the other
neatly folded down.
Her other half may be broken
or in a rummage elsewhere.
Does he pad in slippers to the fridge
and does he gaze into the Coldspot light,
his two black dots on a cheese
or remains of a rack of lamb?

There is a sleek blue seal (salt)
on a sleek blue drum of pepper.
He balances his ball but it's all
so slick for a circus seal.
There is a single maraca from Fla.—
we're to shake the pepper to a music!
And ears of corn rising *déshabillé*
from silken tassels and husks.
And a barn and souvenir silo from Iowa,
and angelfish who swim the air
like proverbs taken from the sea
perplexed and dumb, no, stoic, no,
oh, what is their look, oh, it is
the look of our grandmothers
in America's nursing homes.

Happiest of the lot are the birds—
mated pairs all with two or three
holes in their heads. Bluebirds:
He of widespread wings under
which She may nest or not,
as her seasons declare.

Two parrots, two painted turkeys.
These birds can be made to flock
as the giant woman wishes,
in mock dramas that mingle
their kinds and geographies.
They will fly to each other
all aflutter with joy.
They will circle a letter
that has come, by courier, at last.

And if she wishes they will serve
in the ordinary way: lodged
on a table—sometimes a light,
sometimes a groaning board—
handy for one who wants seasoning.
The domestic job is not work
that works a woman's fingers to the bone.
With a foul rag and a strong soap,
she rubs both salt and pepper to come clean.

# THE DAY LILY AND THE FOX

An Irish soul walks away from Paddy's
late, and the shine on his cap comes
from a long pink neon tube for beer.

He's not drunk, you can see that,
but he misses all the cracks on the walk.
He'll be going home to his mother,

whose back he has not broken,
and to an oilcloth-covered table: flowers,
roosters and yellow checks in the pattern.

When it's warm again he'll be stopping
at Saint Peter's field to see the players
pitch the A-League games at night.

He'll stay by the low fence with the boys
or squeeze, with a sno-cone, into the bleachers.
Paddy's will cream the Harvard Trust Bombers.

The notion is the simple do less harm.
*Do ye no harm* sounds weak until you try,
and find each gesture harms—that a bowl

of cereal leaches the Iowa topsoil away.
Too much or too little adds to the heap
burning on the rubbish islands,

insulated from every soothing rain
(as little harm as the day lily or the fox).
The notion is the meek will inherit,

that ones who watch daylong as jays
twine a nest are pure and holy spirits.
It wouldn't figure that the creative one

would elect the vacant and the sorry,
unless these come into the world to prove
our love—which itself would pull no weight

among the orbits, however popular,
unless it be a striking thing, adaptive
as gills, tendrils, fur or gripping tails.

# THESE I HAVE LOVED

*"These I have loved: White plates
and cups, clean-gleaming."*
RUPERT BROOKE

Ropes hang down from heaven, heavy with apples,
light with plans for plunges into the Big Muddy.
Titans, Rupert, have backed us to the straits;
no little rowboats are coming like fleet stars.
How dare you place teacup, fruit, plate—
these I have loved in oblique late light.
The ninety-three-million-mile light engages
a porcelain glaze and I wanna hold your hand.
Something about having a heart makes it hard
for poker players playing the old gamble.
Let's do tea leaves for the Trilaterals:
brown, banked like loam, cupped in one of our
smoothest achievements, an artifact like the hand...

By George, these leaves say success!
One loaf and one fish in the kitty.

Power could be for something: pan bread,
griddle cakes, a bolt of beautiful cloth.
One more glob of sun melts on the world
and our great goose darkens in its glaze.
Power might be cured of an afternoon.
Take a good look at this tangerine:
poles shrunken like the moon of a violent giant,
puckered at the navel like an old mouth,
rumpled, stippled, flecked, dotted and pricked,
patchy, pointillist and strewn with color:

*this* is the world that is squeezed
until the skin snaps and juice dribbles out.

*Green the Witch-Hazel Wood*
was designed by Tree Swenson.

The cover is by Emily Hiestand
from the series *In the Rainforest*
(oil on canvas, 34 × 34 inches)

The Baskerville type was set by
The Typeworks.

The book was manufactured by
Thomson-Shore.